DIVINITY SCHOOL

DIVINITY SCHOOL

Alicia Jo Rabins

The American Poetry Review
Philadelphia

Cover art: "Initiatory Scene" by Arrington de Dionyso, 2012, acrylic on paper
Book design and composition: VJB/Scribe
Distribution by Copper Canyon Press/Consortium

Alicia Jo Rabins was a participant in Lower Manhattan Cultural Council's
Workspace program. Lower Manhattan Cultural Council empowers artists by
providing them with networks, resources, and support, to create vibrant,
sustainable communities in Lower Manhattan and beyond. LMCC.net

Library of Congress Control Number:
ISBN 978-0-9860938-8-3, cloth
ISBN 978-0-9860938-9-0, paper

9 8 7 6 5 4 3 2

To my parents, with love

CONTENTS

INTRODUCTION

Alicia Rabins's *Divinity School* is a first book of final questions, a book that makes the great mysteries as real as potholes but does not presume to know how to fill them. Nevertheless the need to ask is enormous. She has a means of distillation that projects an impression of light around its object before dissolving back into the surround we must all fumble, grope, stagger through, some with much more determination and clarity than others. Rabins is determined to understand as much as she can while there is time, time that "delay in glass" lodged deeply in unmapped oceans of space.

She wills herself to pay attention knowing the pay-off may not be much more than a wheeze. Though no one looks to her to resolve her quarrel with God or history or suffering or death; no one expects the unsettling wisdom that comes from this continuous interrogation, intense listening or resistant acceptance. No one else could rake so many dreams from so much ash. Old stories, old allegories, myths, sacred and contested texts, old structures broken, perhaps beyond repair, are put in service of the new circumstances that resemble the ones experienced a million and one times before.

Few reliable clues, certainly no prescriptions, move to the front of the line to offer recompense to the unspared faces; the drained and doomed, the drowned ones, the forgotten. Unforsaken wells of love, faith and prayer will never adequately account for the solace of sex, the seas, the days, the moon's silence—including, of course, the golden air, its shiny parts, and the tired dray of beauty.

She is releasing familiar stories from their foxed and fragile pages, not of their creation, but of their sclerotic, gendered subordination; converting them into "a hologram spinning onstage, / white light whipped to cream." Whatever you have longed to know looms into view, and continues to elude in the fog. But a glimpse is more than most of us ever get before it is too late to tell the rest what was just there.

In Alicia Jo Rabins's *Divinity School*, the word is what we have to help us see. Without a scourging blanket of moralizing, the poet sustains a thoughtful, seemingly fundamental inquiry that could lead to a thoughtful engagement with now, when everything roils and troubles as it did for Gaia's first survivors, first casualties. An upturned table is set in the blue sky, and a tippy chair is reserved at the table on earth, and the possibilities reach toward what Carlo Levi termed 'the ancient heart of the future,' to keep it awake and beating. What happens next: after a Jewish woman, a scholar of the Torah, a mother, a singer, a seeker, not a bellwether, but an ardent participant in the whole mess says that waking is seeing, and making a language of what you see is what you are willing to open your eyes to.

How ancient the loneliness
of the young woman in a beet-red skirt
who peers carefully at her phone
while waiting for her coffee
this autumn afternoon.

— C.D. Wright

DIVINITY SCHOOL

Il futuro ha un cuore antico

CARLO LEVI

BLUE TABLE OF SKY

Was it bitterness? *The bitterness*
of iron. Of being a link? *Yes.*
And to what end. *Yes.* But
was it hope? *Sometimes.*
Sorrow or joy? *What difference?*
What else was there? *There was always food.*
Dumplings, tea, fruit. I remember
watching my face change from old woman
to young girl in a basement mirror.
I remember holding my daughter's hand
and seeing my grandmother's visions.
The one who thought her baby
was a bouquet of flowers. *Yes,*
and the wallpaper a map. Did you love
a city? *Many cities.* Did you love
a man? *Many men.* A woman?
A few. Which one do you think of
now? *The husband and the girl*
from high school. I remember
clouds spilling across
the upturned blue table of sky.
I remember black sky white
stars waves moon salt
green streaks beneath
the water. Do you think
we could have known?
I still don't know.

THE DEFINITIONS

As a young girl
I used to study
the definitions.
Body a sphere
that walks around
waterlogged,
eating pretzels with mustard.
Beauty a hologram
spinning onstage,
white light whipped to cream.
Time a crack in a mirror
that changes your face
when you look.

MALKHUT

> That which defines space can stand aloof from space.
> That which defines time, on the other hand, cannot
> remain apart from it.
>
> ARYEH KAPLAN

The field of time stands up
and grows a face.
Arms sprout from his side,
wings from the arms, blue mouth

burning between the feathers.
The field of time changes the air
around him as a sunken pothole
changes the road, as a flaming tree

illuminates the yard. Then
takes a brush and begins
to sketch us: double helix paint
on a canvas of cells.

HOW TO TRAVEL

Sometimes you see the leaves as birds who have traveled all night and come to rest at dawn. Sometimes you feel the space between molecules of honey. Sometimes you are at the airport. Sometimes you are at the hospital. You find your seat an hour before sunrise and watch polar bears swim slowly underwater through the glass. Oh immigration, oh fluorescent lights, the surgeon's rubber gloves, brush-tips of death against your cheek. This country stamps your passport and hands it back forever changed.

THE STORY OF NOAH

What was it like building an ark and leaving some things on the side?
Who watched him pull away from the shore that used to be his hillside rooftop?
He was careful not to think about those eyes too much, those babies.

In the cabin, a raven and a dove slept side by side with branches in their beaks.
His wife was pleasant. His three sons and their wives
were pleasant. The sound of rain the sound of rain the sound of

rain on all sides lulled like the sides of sleep tugging him down.
But when the rain stopped, the rain stopped being a reason.
In the wooden wall of the ark was a tsohar.

This was a. a window b. a glowing precious stone c. we don't know.
Noah looked up and saw. In the wooden wall of Noah there was also a tsohar.
Sometimes the voice of God would come through

and blind everyone in the ark, bouncing against the sides
until it found its way back out to hover over the water.
At a certain point, this all became unbearable: the light,

the raven and the dove, his sons, their wives, and the sense that the sea outside
was boiling. And so he flung the stone into the water.
And so when Noah let all the birds go Noah was letting Noah go.

He flew out of his own tsohar away from his wife and ark.
Away from all the people who died because he did not save them.
Away from the years lost to rain and slumber.
I want to know what happened then.

HOW YOU CAME TO BE

Swear you'll go as deep
as you possibly can, my wife said
before I set out on the submarine voyage.
I promised her and donned my gear.
The paparazzi followed me down,
but one by one they drowned.
Starfish nibbled at their flesh
and little bubbles rose cheerfully,
heralding their demise.
I was too busy to notice,
for I was occupied
with a great responsibility:
dials and switches,
and four men's lives in my hands.
We went deeper and deeper
until the pressure was like
trying to stay alive one day past
your destined death-hour
in order to attend your daughter's wedding.
It took tremendous will
just to breathe down there.
But the thought of you
in that imaginary wedding dress
got me through.
Ohhhhh my daughter.
When we had reached our target depth
we began a careful ascent.
Look!, one of my men said,
and pointed to my erection.
But I was not ashamed.

By then I knew that this whole journey
had existed to prepare me
for the moment later that night
when I would bury myself
in the deepest depths of your mother.

THE MAGIC

My students visit me in the basement.
I hand each one a small well
of ground-up letters
the color of crushed pearl,
a cream base for lids.
We study the magic of powder,
shadow, wand, brush
till beauty beats their faces
with its little tendrils
and red butterflies
settle on their cheeks.
Let my thighs sag, girls,
let my belly distend.
Let me teach you about beauty:
a slanted shipwreck
draped in its own torn sails.

FISH POETICA

The pool of the soul is deep,
maybe infinite.
I cast my line
and the fish I find:
beautiful rainbow fish
yellow stinking fish
with no eyes
and sometimes no fish
just the feeling
of plummet.

THE MAN IN THE EARTH ROOM

The man in the earth room takes care of the earth room
He tends the soft brown the soft soil the soft beautiful brown soil
Where I am eager to lie down and for the first time I do not fear it
I once lived on a street far away from here called Rechov Shabazi

It featured the usual ball-playing etc. but also a rust which seemed to signify
Rusted squares tacked onto the sides of buildings like an industrial quilt
Buildings full of small children eating and singing and riding tricycles around the balconies
Why am I telling you this

It seemed to signify ancient-ness I don't know it felt like a clue
Something you might need to know later on
That the darkest brown of that rust
Not the reddish end not the continuum between red and brown but the single darkest spots

Were the same as the brown of the earth room
As the brown eyes of the earth room's caretaker
He would let you in if it was your birthday
Even if it were not technically a day the earth room was open

Because when the city fogs over   locks you out
And you are stuck wandering around downtown
You can come in and breathe the quiet expanse of crumbly dark brown earth
The quiet expanse of your own eventual grave

Meanwhile the caretaker eats his soup behind the white privacy wall
And do you know why angels eat soup
Because it does not crunch
Soup is another one of those hints of the afterlife

Scattered like blossoms through this mess of days
Every once in a while I try to gather an armful of them
And lay them on the desk of the caretaker as a gift when he is not looking
Although I know he sees me whether he is looking or not

ATITLÁN

Green volcanoes
embrace the lake.
Each afternoon
the xocomil comes,
wind that rubs the lake
against its grain.
Then sunset broadens
the view.
The first time
we stand captivated,
but soon even breathing
becomes commonplace
and evening an exercise
of willing myself
to pay attention.
You say, "I want to get
drunk tonight!"
And then you buy
two boxes of wine
from Don Rafa, and do.
I am far from home.
I want to be a good traveller.
I have come here to love you.
I hold you as you wheeze
in your sleep.

BETWEEN THE TONGUE AND THE WARM SALT

Dearling. Sweatheart.
In the quantum spaces between words
people understand each other.
They meet in a central square
and have a hot pretzel.
They taste the same salt.
Don't be scared because
we are ghosts to each other.
I'm sorry I will leave you.
Put your finger inside me. Taste my salt.
We snap at each other
while bombs kill people elsewhere.
You put on a skirt and ride your bicycle away.
I'm sorry! I shout.
When you turn around at the corner
and start riding back,
two journals will merge:
the one I'm writing now, from birth to death,
and the one my life's writing backwards.
Their lines appear to cross
but a scientist would see space
howling between the tongue
and the warm salt.

TOO LATE

It is too late. Late to uncreate light,
to take back what's been said and,
wet wind, late to be out trawling for a baby:
the sea black, the floodlight pouring.
I stroke my feathered throat on the captain's deck,
weighing seconds and decades,
spoils of antiquity. Home at last
I am soaked. Drained. Wrung out.
I stick a chicken in the oven, I stick
both my hands in it and cry,
"Cook us both together God, if you are going to!"
It is a quarrel of lifelong friends.
God and I understand each other —

we are both very old. We both know
it is late for me to might have been,
to magic-wand muteness to life, just as God
cannot unmultiply, defruit, divide,
undo dominion, close rib-flesh over, thumb
continents together, unsplit upper & lower,
watercolor all firmament, all hovering.
Bodiless breath. Too late, God,
for both of us. Waste and wild, too late.

HOW TO GRADUATE

God wrote me a letter in invisible ink. But I got overwhelmed:
the parchment, the lemon juice the light and the candle. I
accidentally set it on fire. For forty days and nights, the smell
of caramel surrounded me, and when it receded, I sent out
my only dove.

DEAR EARTH ROOM MAN

I am finally mailing you the letter I wrote you
Ten years ago when I breathed in the earth room
There's a privilege to marriage and a privilege
To being 26 and single I've seen it a dozen times

That flowering

It happened to me dear Earth Room Man
You don't know me but I've been thinking about you
For ten years ever since that day with Jen
Halfway between our birthdays when

I wasn't afraid of death for the first time

In your presence
Burial felt like a soft brown flower
A wedding dress I would wear one day
If I was lucky and if that's true

We're all lucky Earth Room Man

In that letter I said you were an angel
But I know that was my imagination
You are a man at a desk like any other but beside
The desk is a room full of brown earth

And I think you've grown wise from that

Day after day breathing in the earth room
And today I'm sending you two letters
Ten years apart have you ever I hope you have
I hope you have a good life I've been thinking
Of you

HOW TO TELL TIME

Now,
like manna,
is perfectly
sufficient
and will rot
if stored.

HOW TO CROSS-COUNTRY SKI

Bring whiskey. The snowflakes are tiny pillows; the snowflakes are white dots. Together they add up to a field for you to plow with your feet. You are a giant. You are in another country. Your thigh muscles are newborn mice. Listen: it is the silence of a houseful of sleepers. It's a moon silence. Read the snow while it scrolls across the hills. It's in the static. You'll never get it again exactly like this.

DIVINITY SCHOOL

I kept thinking about suffering
and how until I look at it there is no movement.
Wanting to be better than you, and all that.
I thought the monastery would save me
from myself, but the timpani beat there
in my stone room,
the flutes performed their demonic runs
and at night, I felt women's fingers crawling
beneath my robes.

So I moved to this cabin.
I live alone with a bed,
some clothes, and the demons who know me best.
I knit hats for us all.
Once you've had beauty,
it's hard to let it go.
Now I remember why I ran
from the Ancients.

HOW TO SING

A nightmare has wings.
You sleep in the death camp
with tiny feathers on your face.
You wake up near the mineral pools.
A singer must paint her nightmare directly
onto the dream of her listeners
until it becomes the listener's dream.
Then rescue the dreamer
who wakes up wet with tears.

MY DESIRE FOR THE SUPERMODEL VS. MY DESIRE FOR THE 50-YEAR-OLD EXPERT ON ARCANE LANGUAGES

It's a lonely life mostly. The exceptions are, well,
exceptions. I could make myself cry but I think
it's the onions. I try to make a home environment
where you can both sit with me.
Sit next to me.
I live in the white part of town.
All the pictures on my walls are of white people.
There is a place where we close ourselves off to each other.
You, sweet Kate, are a rock star.
A green shoot piercing my heart from the inside.
And you, Mr. Wolf, your eyes hold a pooled
liquid which I want to make spill over.
Every city is lonely at night.
The country also. Lonely at night.
I followed that loneliness into the corner of my hipbones.
Got down on my knees and fed it little bits of pastry.
Jesus, I am almost
as old as my own grandmother.
I am on my knees, shoving bits of pastry
up my cunt.
Thank you God for that word, cunt.
Or perhaps I should say thank you cunt for that word, God.
They are both wrapped around my finger.
Let me know if you need directions to my house.

THE STORY OF JONAH

You have to get in your car. You have to go to work.
You have to feed yourself like a child: balanced,
on schedule. Otherwise you end up on your office floor,

thrown overboard by high-waisted women who peer down
at you, calling you "bad luck," calling you "storm."
This morning you turned on your computer and saw

a blank quilt square that used to be filled with words.
"What confuses me," you say, "is that the computer
only does what you tell it to." You have to look

at the Christmas lights to keep spirits up,
where they are wound, on the high lampposts.
Look up at the rows of boxes to buy: toilet paper,

crackers, tea. On the office floor, there is nothing
to be a professor of. The sailors cast their dice
of disapproval down like flowers

shaking their pollen. You watch their face-petals shrink
and fall off. You lie on the office floor covered
with women. You sit up. You promise never

to run away again. You carry your computer to your car.

HOW TO ASSESS YOUR NET WORTH

Take two small pieces of paper. On one, write: *the world was created for me*. On the other: *I am only dust and ashes*. Put one in each pocket. Never leave the house without them.

THE SEPARATION COURSE

In the gold room I am golden.
In the jade room I am jade.
In the infrared room I am silent.
In the cold plunge I am mute.

Meet me at the sushi bar
panorama window, where we
dangle bright pink slabs of tuna
above our mouths, studying dolphin.

A bird from outside lives inside me;
I snuck her in. I keep her eggs
in my belly to warm them, and we animals,
having been ice, having been jade, are changed.

When the ripening course
is complete, the separation
course begins. An ice land
must be entered alone—

without even you my love.
I lay my forehead to the frozen wall.
I see death, I see profit,
a pink stone, a piece of jade

in the hand, a piece of gold
to carry in the dark.

HOW TO BE A PROPHET

There is a frozen waterfall
at a man's center.
Your job is to kneel
below, to warm
his body, to draw
that slow fountain
into your mouth,
like a prophet
receiving God's word.

HOW TO MAKE A GIRL COME

Think of friends who died young. In other words, a candle
hangs in the dark womb. Your job is to light the candle with
your deepest match. A wick connects your heart to your fin-
gers; along this string, fire travels. The ends of your fingers
become four little skulls longing for the grave of her body.
This is the grave of winter, when spring moistens the soil.
Once that happens, it is easy to let go of winter.

INVOCATION TO CHARLOTTE, GODDESS OF THE TARMAC

From seat 12A I call to you,
God in the form of Charlotte,
Goddess of the Tarmac.
A roar happens when you're around,
a sibilance of engines unlocks
all the heart's granaries.
Charlotte sings
love songs
to Charlotte,
and everybody wants to sleep with her
because she points to you.
It's her deep voice
and the chaos she holds together
with the ribbons pinned to her mannish suit.
She's nourished by propriety
and fed by the forbidden.
Sometimes she presses my shoulder
to make me sit down;
sometimes says to me,
sweetie, drink seltzer, it'll settle your stomach — but
there's no seltzer left
because we're stuck in an airplane on the runway
and we won't be allowed to leave for hours, possibly days
and I can see the edges of kindness unravelling
in myself and everyone else;
allegiances form
and prejudices are confirmed
and all our kidneys are taut with the smell of oncoming conflict.
Which is why I invoke
you at this moment,

God in the form of Charlotte,
Goddess of the Tarmac,
to whom I pray,
please
open the small door
with its rounded edges
and let us out
before we murder each other.

SISTER

Knowing is a mockery
if we cannot know each other
and a mockery if we do.
She woke me up screaming
each night while she slept,
and I held myself apart from her dreams
like a lover or a surgeon,
she was a fisherman's wife
ripping nets in the evening
and mending them in the morning.
When she grew older she carried
a dildo in a black plastic bag,
always piercing the lyric
with some kind of symptom
while her hair hung low over
the orange blossoms she painted,
her eyes angled up
towards the sanitarium jars
she arranged on shelves.
There is a temptation to eulogize
that which I do not understand
and to think of a sister as a thing
that should be beautiful.
A thing that does not bleed
at night. Whose horrors
are lesser than or equal to my
own. As if I could know
my own.

HERE ARE THE CLUES

The refrigerator sighs at night
while the house is sleeping.
The provolone cheese just sits there,
sits, sits, sits, until someone picks it up.
But tiny invisible changes are happening
and if it sits long enough it grows
a little garden on its yellow plain.
And me, oh, I too sit sit sit,
waiting for someone. And my changes
are also imperceptible.
I put on my scarf, then take it off.
I stare into the cold glow, pricing plane tickets,
click click click, but I don't buy.
I wash my face and brush my teeth.
All night while the house sleeps
the kitchen clock reaches out to strike
the refrigerator's white cheek.

HOW THE DINOSAURS DIED

It's no big deal to wake up
and carry a satchel with the death
of the dinosaurs in it
all day.

While elsewhere a person
metamorphosizes into a soldier
the meadow of his mind
torn up day by day

to protect those like me
who dream of dinosaurs
and wake up to write it down
in the too-late morning.

What does the soldier dream?
Did the smoke from my dream reach him too
or did he dream of
prom queens and ribbons.

I am sorry, soldier,
dinosaurs, ocean.
I am not the smoke that kills you.
But I am part of the smoke.

HOW TO CONFESS AN AFFAIR

Details are fishhooks that will remain in the lip of the small fish that lives inside your spouse and swims sometimes towards you, sometimes away from you. If you love the fish, be careful.

THE MATTER OF LOVE

Ugly husbands hide in holes,
dug by handsome wives.
Subtle foxes play their roles
and then break out in hives
while priests delineate the goals
and drinkers drink in dives.
Girls wind garlands round the poles
that boys have carved with knives,
old men warm themselves at coals
that used to be their brides.
And so it is, the road goes on,
and on the body drives,
'til undertakers take our souls,
and throw away our lives.

A GARDEN AGAINST SUICIDE

I plant ivy and lavender
I tie a note on the sparrow's back

Please don't drink the poison wine
Think of the pumpkin patch by the side of the highway

The magazine of the seasons
The sparrow flies out the window

October contains a hint of March
The garden wears a vest of mint leaves

For you she tosses her head of lettuce
Her vagina lined with pomegranate seeds

Her face lined with your face

BIRTH

I found myself in a dark room
pregnant, and alone.
No midwife, no telephone.
Then the demons found me.

They crowded round and crowed.
Sweet demons, fuck you all,
I said as I stretched and pushed and kicked.
What else could I say?

They flooded the dark red walls.
I asked them to help.
What else could I do?
And one by one,

they placed their hands on my belly
and began to chant.
And so it was that you were born,
little monster with my face.

I swear the demons cried
as they held you up
to the light.

CHUTE

Each time a baby is born
the universe squeezes itself
through a chute,
the same chute
into which
suicides squeeze themselves.
Its mouth
is lined with small iron teeth.
When you bathe your father
who has become like a child,
you feel the teeth
on your fingers.
When your father asks
who you are,
it means his legs have been
sucked in.
For you the tunnel's
mouth is closed.
For him it is open
and oiled.

A VACCINATION FOR LONELINESS

O Lord, the praise on my tongue
has turned to fear.
I think
you are afraid too.
Can't the street vendor sell us back
our salty
hot pretzel?
Can't the scientists
make a vaccination
for this kind of loneliness?
Can't the monks
teach us
to build a sailboat
out of all this broken wood?

WILLOW

I was fifteen
when you called me woman,
we toasted *to the adolescent I was.*
Like a pair of exotic fruits
that could not breed
when placed together.
Beauty.
In a casket made of willow.
I could not beat it.
I could not bear it.
Time the adulterer:
a delay in glass, a decay.

VOXEL

How ancient the loneliness
of the young woman in a beet-red skirt
who peers carefully at her phone
while waiting for her coffee
this autumn afternoon.
She watches the room collapse to a small box,
a smaller box, and finally a dot.
The dot is the size of a fertilized egg.
It's where a thought begins.
In the laboratory of night
where we open again and again
for the scientists to confirm
our wiring. You are elsewhere,
hand on your phone.
How long before we understand each other?
How long before we meet?

FLORIDA

There are beautiful girls out there on the beach
like baubles on the world's wrist.
I'm surprised when they let me kiss them. (Rarely).
But I'm lucky, I tell myself all the time. You're lucky,
it's very important that you understand how lucky you are:
don't help me write this letter, just step back
and think about it for a minute.
What you call lonely, someone else would call "not-hungry,"
"not-afraid-for-my-life."
So why are you crying, dear I?
There's a seashell I want to pick up. I want to stick my tongue
in its salty whorls. Yes, it hurts to want,
doesn't it. It never stops hurting.
And you'll never be comfortable in Florida:
long thin land of bathing suits and alligators,
the whole state a charm bracelet
on the wrist of a girl
you're not supposed to touch.

THE MERMAID MURDERED BY TIME

A mermaid crawls out of my mouth to meet you in this poem,
my teacher who calls me teacher and therefore is my teacher,
who shows me how to knot a net to make the moon rise
during night watch on calm seas while the other sailors sleep.

We are the ocean and our speaking the waves, each phrase
a little breaker spreading its foam. "A poem is a scrimshaw knife,"
you tell me. "The carved pictures mean something and the blade
cleans a fish for dinner." "But why can't the poem be the fish?"

"Because the fish will die." By now we've knotted a net
that covers the deck, and the moon is up. "Oh teacher,
I feel so far from New York." "Well, teacher, we are.
Out here we eat of the sea and navigate by star." You teach me

to throw the mind into the water and haul it in full of frantic poems,
choosing which to keep and which to fling back quickly,
while they slap themselves in panic against the cold wood.
We pick the best two for a meal and eat them raw. And now

that we are satisfied, you say, let us lie back and read a poem
of the constellations. Orion contains the future: there is a stellar
nursery in his sword. Unlike you, I am patient, Orion says,
stretched out on his rack though he was there far before

medieval torture and, in fact, is not there at all. Who
is more imaginary, me or Orion? Is it wrong to toss the word "torture"
around like a shiny fish while people are locked in cells?
Should we try to imagine them? My teacher and I look

at each other for a few hours. It's a problem,
this incarnational merry-go-round, some humans on a poem-boat
in the middle of the ocean and some children begging for food
from tourists and some in jail for having murdered a girl.

I could say it's the mermaid murdered by time, but it's wrong
to redeem cruelty for beauty, isn't it, teacher? Teacher,
why are you silent?

GOODBYE, DREAM OF THE GOLDEN WEST

Angels are not beings a wave passed through once. Not pale ladies not perfect forms stretched out on a plastic pool-chair in late morning like a white shark on a bed of lettuce, plated for the eyes. It's not forever ten o'clock on the sundial of the pool. A woman does not turn into an angel with a click. I don't believe her shoulder would be warm against my hand if I came to surprise her. I don't believe she's waiting for me.

HOW TO SAIL

Scrape the curse off the parchment. Stir the broken letters
into a jar of water. Make a woman drink it: thus said Elo-
him. But why: thus said Molly, twelve years old. Now I was
the teacher. We sat there, two black flames in a room of white
fire. We were sailing on a wind that passed through the open
window of a room next to the marketplace, two thousand
years ago.

DEAD SEA SCROLLS

At the beach
you tell me
your father is
dead but not
how he died.
He's a dead
sea scroll and
you are too.
You've been
rolled up for
thousands of years.
You have to be taken out
of your clay
jar carefully, with
tweezers. Funny
how time is both destroyer
and preserver,
well not funny but
strange. When air
and sunlight touch
those ancient letters
they disintegrate.
I want to go
back in time and say
to myself
be careful,
you are already
beginning to love
what's written
there.

HORSE POETICA

My horse looks like a few red streaks
someone painted in the air.
I'm always surprised when she holds my weight.
Yes
sometimes I feel sick and have to lie down for days.
It hurts when the road goes on without me
to destinations which will vanish before I arrive.
It hurts to be sick, to grow old with a child's heart.
But the sky is too shiny to hold night for long.
And when the sickness drains there she is again,
gesturing towards the act of motion,
kicking the dust into little red clouds.

AT THE SCHOOL FOR YOUNG UNICORNS

Our training involved LSD and cathedral nights
A difficult preparation for extinction in tapestries
Gold, forest green, burgundy, dark blue
We dreamed of immortality
We flexed our young flanks
We practiced beauty on each other
We slept in a clearing
We walked barefoot on gravel
We played scales on stringed instruments
We memorized sayings
We learned that wisdom seeks low places
Like water we followed the wisdom
Into the low places
The gates closed

SUNDAY SCHOOL

Look around this cafe, everyone is reading The New York Times and talking,
which all adds up to a clamor of breakfast noises and a mosaic of Sunday papers.
Look at this messy cartoon I call my "life," which does not know
whether it is living or being lived.
It happened again on the way here:
a man looked at me on the subway, directly, meaningfully, brazenly.
This is a different way of being a woman,
which I always disdained, complained, refrained from and now
something must cry look at me, look at me!
And the thrill of being looked-at quivers me to attention.
Being noticed, like noticing, has a sharp blade.
I too cannot help but notice all the beautiful women who populate this restaurant,
it seems they are too beautiful to possibly be real;
and what is it all for anyway, all this ungraspable perfection, because
although right now their beauty is as full as a ripe boysenberry,
crushable, staining, straining their own edges, aching
to be popped in the mouth and tasted
(and they offer it as such)
soon it will be over, their beauty, and only the desire will remain.
All the fucking in the world never erases desire,
and moreover it creates a Next Generation with desire of their own.
So any cessation of desire becomes futile, impossible.
And so we keep putting on our strappy heels day after day,
just "not feeling right" if we wear sneakers or flip flops,
offering ourselves up for this one day:
offering our beauty on the altar of this particular Sunday
like a coffee and a newspaper, to be swallowed and read
and left behind on the cafe table,
leaving faint black smudges on our one-day-older fingertips.

TAJ MAHAL

I wish I could tell you
how it was at the festival
you had your eyes closed and I
had mine open beneath
the clustered blackberries
that hung over us like exploding
stars. The vines had climbed
up a tree I don't know
what kind of tree it was
and now I'm so far away
I'll never know. You can get
eye surgery and visit the Taj Mahal
and it will still be cheaper
than it would have been here,
so don't worry about the great
distances there are airplanes
to take us to each other. If you
had opened your eyes you would
have seen in mine your own face
hovering among the blackberries
tart, frightening and immediate.

HOW TO MAKE A RED VELVET CAKE

Drink until the kitchen blurs. Recall the papier-mâché volcano you made. Lean over the counter. Cry into the batter. My precious vial of red, when you are making this cake, you are blood and bones—red blood, white bones, grease the pan, beware.

HOW TO COUNT BONES

In the hospital, when everyone leaves for the night, I climb
up the string to the kite of your head, back down. Both of
us cut loose from birthdreams. Now you hold those dreams
in your miniature girl hands. Your first indignant cry on the
other side of the blue sheet. Square face in a triangle hat as
your father held you to the light. You origami, you blueprint,
mine. Like peas, or pearls, your spine.

THE YOUNG WOMAN AND THE TINY FOLDS

Who is the young woman?
She contains the five tiny folds.
When is the woman young?
There is time to fold and be folded.
How young is the woman?
Ask Time the seamstress with her miles of yellow thread.
Where does the young woman go?
Elements cannot be fully explained.
What secret gestures do we discreetly pass on?
The five tiny folds of love.

EVENING PRAYER

Dock Lord
your boat at my door
tonight.
The pier's fringe
falls on itself
and is raised by you.
Take my badge of
disbelief,
the scab I forage in,
lift the hammered copper
from my wrists.

With your oceanic hands,
with brief green shoots
and the stubble of lighthouses
with my irrefutable body
please Lord tend
the flogging sheet
of my soul.

Dock Lord
your boat at my door tonight.
I'll be waiting
by the thick black mark
you dug into the wood.
Carry my mistakes on your
shoulders, and unbind
the parcel of my body:

Take away my sticks, stow
my tired speech,
turn me inside out
so my shiny part
faces the sky, so it can
take upon itself all the stars,
all the dumb blue oil of the night.

FLOOD

My consort takes me to see
the cuneiform in the locked,
climate-controlled basement.
He shows his card and the guard
guides us down two flights of stairs
to a small room where we
stand before the delicate stone.
"What does it say?" I ask.
He translates for me: "A great flood
destroyed the world. The world
grew back. A great flood
destroyed the world again.
The world grew back again.
When will the flood come back?
Soon, soon." Together
we ride the elevator up to the ground
floor and step out
into the golden air.

NOTES

"Malkhut"
Malkhut, literally "dominion," is the worldly emanation of divine presence according to the kabbalistic mystics. It is associated with the Shechina, the feminine manifestation of God.

"The Story of Noah"
Tsohar is, as the poem says, a difficult word to translate because it appears in only one place in the Torah, the story of Noah. It gives light to the ark; interpretations range from a window to a magically illuminating gemstone.

"Atitlán"
Lago de Atitlán is a lake in Guatemala, created by a volcanic crater, ringed with volcanoes, and considered sacred by the local Mayan communities. Each afternoon a wind passes over the lake; this wind is called, in Mayan, *xocomil*. X is pronounced "sh".

"How To Assess Your Net Worth" is based on a Chassidic teaching.

"Evening Prayer" was commissioned by composer S. Beth May.

ACKNOWLEDGMENTS

Many thanks to the magazines and anthologies in which these poems previously appeared:

6×6: "Divinity School" (as "This Cabin"), "Fish Poetica"

American Poetry Review: "How to Assess Your Net Worth," "How to Graduate," "How To Sing"

Augury Books: "Chute"

A Book of Uncommon Prayer (Outpost19): "Evening Prayer"

Broken Land: Poems of Brooklyn (NYU Press): "Sunday School" (as "Sunday Café")

Collagist: "How to Be a Prophet," "How to Confess an Affair," "How to Make a Red Velvet Cake"

Cortland Review: "The Definitions," "The Magic," "Willow" (as "Sotah's School of Beauty")

Court Green: "My Desire for the Supermodel...," "The Story of Noah"

The Forward: "Flood," "Malkhut"

Horse Poems anthology (Knopf/Everyman's): "Horse Poetica"

Ilanot Review: "How to Sail," "Long Division"

New Delta Review: "How to Travel" (winner of the 2013 Matt Clark Poetry Prize)

On Earth As It Is: "A Vaccination for Loneliness"

Ploughshares: "How You Came to Be," "The Mermaid Murdered by Time"

Poetica: "Too Late"

Sentence: "How to Cross Country Ski," "How to Make a Girl Come"

Squawkback: "How the Dinosaurs Died"

My profound gratitude and love to those without whom this book would not exist. It has been a long road and I cannot name everyone whose fingerprints, stories and pens have touched these pages, but know you are in my heart. In particular, my deepest thanks to C.D. Wright, for selecting this manuscript and for her poems; to the wonderful Elizabeth Scanlon and *American Poetry Review*, and to Michael Wiegers and Copper Canyon. This book would not exist without Filip Marinovich, interstellar poetry chavruta, and Gabrielle Calvocoressi, profound poetic friend. Thank you both. Thanks and deep love to my fellow-travelers in art and friendship, up the alphabet: Colette Alexander, Jonathan Allen, Malinda Ray Allen, Kate Angus, David Freeman, Jen P. Harris, Aaron Hartman, Jascha Hoffman, Corrie Beth Hogg, Vanessa Hua, Kerry Huang, Annette Ezekiel Kogan, Jesse Lichtenstein, Matthew Olzmann, Abigail Susik, Ruth Wikler-Luker. Thanks to Arrington de Dionyso for the beautiful cover art, Lucinda Roanoke for photography, and Valerie Brewster for design. To Megan Wechsler, Dillon Sussman and Kendra Rosenblatt for enduring friendship. To my teachers of writing, music, and Torah; too many to name here, but special thanks to Tony Hoagland, Kenneth Koch z"l, Maurice Manning, Claudia Rankine, & Mary Ruefle. Gratitude to Elizabeth T. Gray Jr, Maeve Kinkead, J.J. Penna, Maggie Schwed and Abby Wender, writing group extraordinaire. To Ross White and the Grind Daily Writing Series. To Peter Avniel Salzman z"l, who taught me about divinity. To Jenny Boully and the New Delta Review for selecting "How to Travel" for the 2013 Matt Clark Poetry Contest. To Lower Manhattan Cultural Council, especially Melissa Levin. To the Covenant Foundation and the Joshua Venture Group for invaluable support. To Ellen Bryant Voigt and the Warren Wilson MFA Program, in gratitude; to Michael Collier and the Bread Loaf Writers Conference, three times over; the Pardes Institute for Jewish Studies, Jerusalem. To Karen, Peter, Stephanie and Nora Rabins, with love fundamental and inexpressible. Penultimate but ultimate, to the Divine, for literally Everything. And to Aaron, Sylvia and Elijah Hartman: you are the loves of my life.

ABOUT THE AUTHOR

Alicia Jo Rabins is a poet, composer, performer and Torah teacher. Alicia was born in Portland, Oregon, grew up in Baltimore, lived in New York City for many years, and now lives in Portland with her husband and two small children.